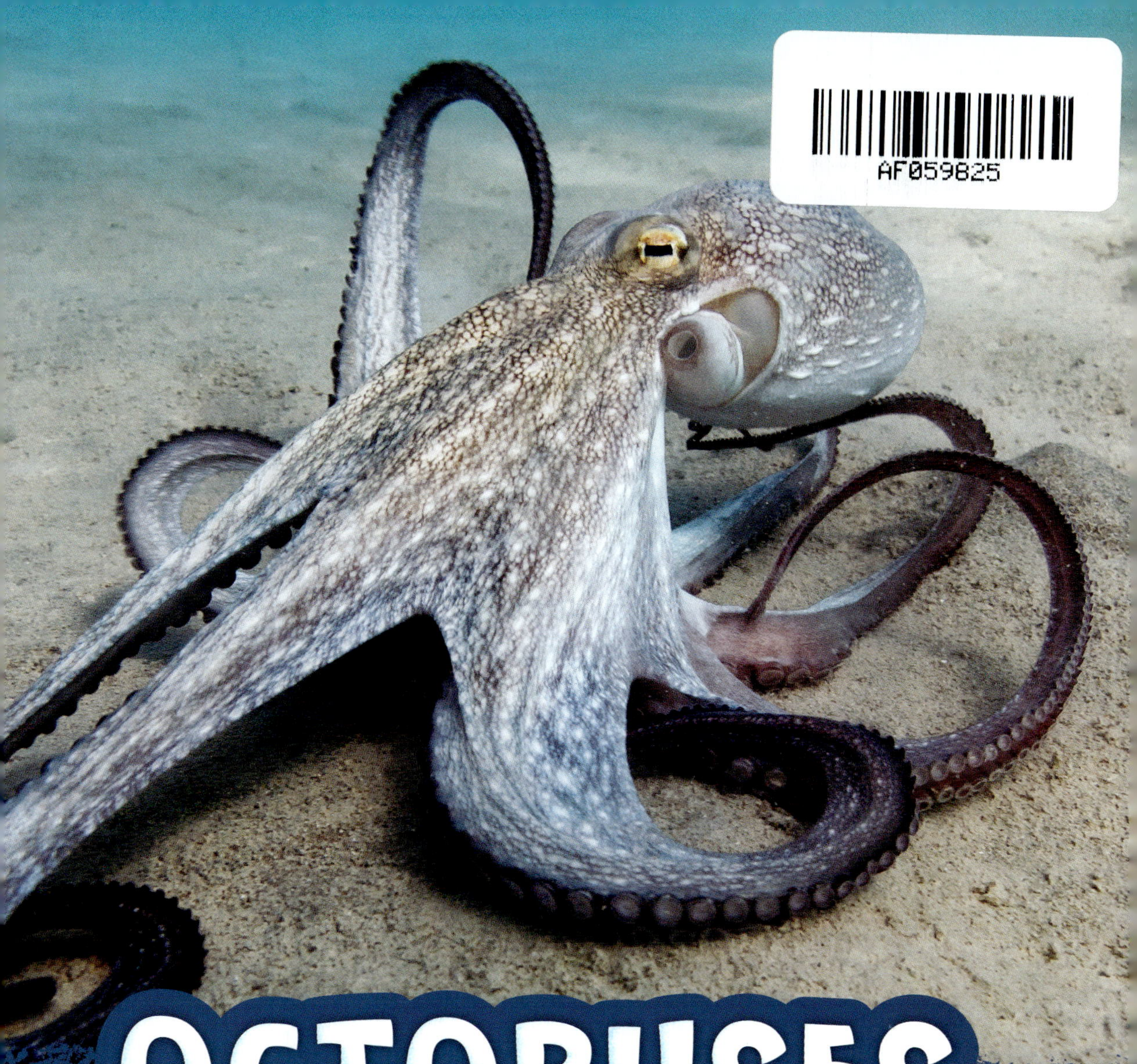

OCTOPUSES

by Jaclyn Jaycox

raintree
a Capstone company — publishers for children

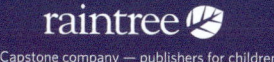

Raintree is an imprint of Capstone Global Library Limited, a company incorporated in England and Wales having its registered office at 264 Banbury Road, Oxford, OX2 7DY – Registered company number: 6695582

www.raintree.co.uk
myorders@raintree.co.uk

Hardback edition text © Capstone Global Library Limited 2023
Paperback edition text © Capstone Global Library Limited 2024

The moral rights of the proprietor have been asserted. All rights reserved. No part of this publication may be reproduced in any form or by any means (including photocopying or storing it in any medium by electronic means and whether or not transiently or incidentally to some other use of this publication) without the written permission of the copyright owner, except in accordance with the provisions of the Copyright, Designs and Patents Act 1988 or under the terms of a licence issued by the Copyright Licensing Agency, 5th Floor, Shackleton House, 4 Battle Bridge Lane, London, SE1 2HX (www.cla.co.uk). Applications for the copyright owner's written permission should be addressed to the publisher.

ISBN 978 1 3982 2492 6 (hardback)
ISBN 978 1 3982 2491 9 (paperback)

Image Credits
Alamy: FLPA, 16; Capstone Press, 6; Newscom: Dave Fleetham, 23, Design Pics/Dave Fleetham, 25, Flip Nicklin, 21; Shutterstock: Andrea Izzotti, 28, Bass Supakit, 19, 22, Cathy Withers-Clarke, 24, Daniel Lamborn, 8, 11, ennar0, 1, 7, Joe Belanger, 5, Kondratuk Aleksei, 10, Konrad Mostert, 13, Konstantin Novikov, 26, Mana Photo, Cover, Martin Voeller, 9, Rich Carey, 18, Richard Whitcombe, 15, Takayuki Ohama, 12

Editorial Credits
Editor: Hank Musolf; Designer: Dina Her; Media Researcher: Morgan Walters; Production Specialist: Tori Abraham

All internet sites appearing in back matter were available and accurate when this book was sent to press.

British Library Cataloguing in Publication Data
A full catalogue record for this book is available from the British Library.

Printed and bound in India.

Contents

Amazing octopuses 4

Where in the world 6

Octopus bodies 8

On the menu 14

Life of an octopus 18

Threats to octopuses 24

Fast facts 29

Glossary 30

Find out more 31

Index 32

Words in **bold** are in the glossary.

Amazing octopuses

A strange-looking animal lives deep in the ocean. It crawls along the ocean floor on eight long arms. What is it? An octopus!

Octopuses don't have backbones. These types of animals are called **invertebrates**. Octopuses are one of the cleverest animals in the world. There are about 300 different types of them.

Where in the world

Octopuses are found in every ocean on Earth. Many live in warm water. They are usually small. Those that live in cold water are much larger.

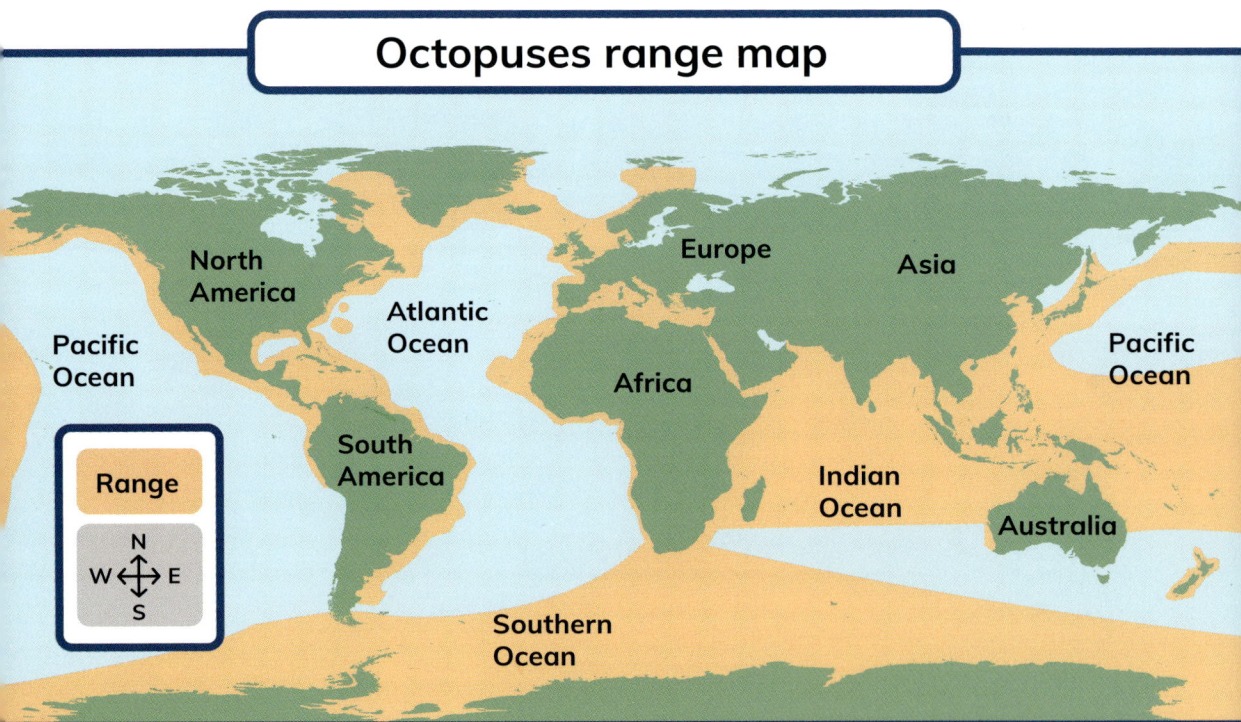

Octopuses range map

Some types of octopuses live near the surface of the water. But most are found on the ocean floor. They live in dens that they make out of rocks.

Octopus bodies

Octopuses are many different sizes. The smallest is the Octopus wolfi. It is less than 2.5 centimetres (1 inch) long. This tiny octopus could sit on your finger!

Octopus wolfi

giant Pacific octopus

The giant Pacific octopus is the largest octopus. On average it weighs about 50 kilograms (110 pounds). It grows about 4.9 metres (16 feet) long. Some can grow even bigger. The largest one ever seen was 9 m (30 feet) across!

Octopuses have big heads. Their head holds their brain, stomach and three hearts. These animals crawl more than they swim. Swimming makes them very tired! When they swim, one of their hearts stops beating.

An octopus' mouth is called a beak. It's the only hard part on its body.

Octopuses have no bones. They are very squishy. They can squeeze into tiny spaces.

Octopuses have eight strong arms. Each one has more than 200 **suckers** on it. The suckers can taste what they touch.

suckers

Octopuses are masters at hiding. They can change the colour of their skin. Doing this helps them blend into things around them. They can even change the feel of their skin. They can make it bumpy or smooth. It makes them almost impossible to see.

On the menu

An octopus reaches into a dark hole. Its arm feels around. Suddenly, it touches something tasty. Snatch! It is time for dinner!

Some octopuses hunt at night. They have great eyesight, even in the dark. Others hunt at sunrise and sunset. Octopuses eat crabs and lobsters. They eat shrimp and fish too.

Octopuses are good hunters. Many drop down on their **prey** from above. They catch them in the webbing between their arms. Then they grab them. Their suckers hold on tightly.

Octopuses bite their prey. Their **saliva** is poisonous. It makes the prey stay still. Then it is easier for them to eat it. Their strong beaks can break hard shells. They tear off chunks of meat and swallow it whole.

Life of an octopus

Octopuses live alone. They only come together to **mate**. Males usually die a couple of months later.

Females lay eggs in their dens. They keep eggs hidden from **predators**. They can lay 200,000 to 400,000 at once. The females then stop eating. They spend all their time protecting the eggs. They keep them clean.

Some types of octopus eggs take only a month or two to hatch. Others take up to 10 months. The females die soon after. The babies must take care of themselves.

The babies are very small at birth. They quickly swim towards the surface. The babies float there with other small animals. This is a dangerous time for them. There are lots of predators. Many won't survive.

Octopuses that make it past this stage grow quickly. They eat tiny plants and animals. When the babies grow big enough, they sink back down to the ocean floor.

Octopuses live short lives. They can only lay eggs once. They usually only live one to three years. Then they die. Some larger types may live a little bit longer.

Threats to octopuses

Octopuses have many predators. Seals, large fish and whales hunt them. Sea otters, eels and birds do too. But octopuses have ways of escaping them.

ink cloud

When an octopus is in danger, it squirts a cloud of ink into the water. The ink makes it hard for other animals to see. They can't taste or smell either. This gives the octopus time to get away.

Octopuses can blow water out of their bodies through a tube. Doing this shoots them backwards, away from the danger. Zoom! They can travel up to 40 kilometres (25 miles) per hour for a short time.

If a predator catches them, it's still not too late. Octopuses may lose an arm to escape. But it's not gone forever. A new arm will grow in its place.

Oil and rubbish also threaten octopuses. The **pollution** makes the sea dirty. It can make them ill. It can also kill the animals they eat. Octopuses may not have enough food. But people are working to help. They are cleaning up the ocean. They want to make it a safe place for these animals to live.

Fast facts

Name: octopus

Habitat: ocean

Where in the world: Pacific, Atlantic, Indian, Arctic and Southern oceans

Food: shrimp, lobster, crabs, fish

Predators: seals, large fish, whales, sea otters, eels, birds

Life span: 1 to 3 years

Glossary

invertebrate an animal without a backbone

mate when a male and female come together to produce young

pollution materials that harm the Earth's water, air and land

predator an animal that hunts other animals for food

prey an animal hunted by another animal for food

saliva the clear liquid in the mouth

sucker a soft, flexible part on an animal's body that is used to cling on to something

Find out more

Books

Blue Planet II, Leisa Stewart-Sharpe (BBC Children's Books, 2020)

Endangered Oceans (Endangered Earth), Jody S. Rake (Raintree, 2020)

Octopuses (The World of Ocean Animals), Bizzy Harris (Pogo Books, 2022)

Websites

National Geographic Kids: Octopus facts
www.natgeokids.com/uk/discover/animals/sea-life/octopus-facts/

YouTube: BBC Earth Kids video
www.youtube.com/watch?v=VmioYqZYBaI

Index

arms 4, 12, 14, 17, 27

beaks 11, 17

eggs 19, 20, 23
eyesight 14

heads 10
hearts 10
hiding 13
hunting 14, 17, 24

ink 25
invertebrates 4

mating 18

pollution 28
predators 19, 20, 24, 27
prey 17

saliva 17
size 8, 9, 20
skin 13
suckers 12, 17
swimming 10, 20

young 20, 22